LITERATURE

THE FAITHFUL LEARNING SERIES

An Invitation to Academic Studies, Jay D. Green

Literature, Clifford W. Foreman

Philosophy, James S. Spiegel

Sociology, Matthew S. Vos

JAY D. GREEN, SERIES EDITOR

LITERATURE

CLIFFORD W. FOREMAN

P&R PUBLISHING
P.O. BOX 817 • PHILLIPSBURG • NEW JERSEY 08865-0817

Scripture quotations are from the Holy Bible, New International Version®, NIV® Copyright © 1973, 1978, 1984, 2011 by Biblica, Inc.® Used by permission. All rights reserved worldwide.

Scripture quotation marked (NRSV) is from New Revised Standard Version Bible, copyright © 1989 National Council of the Churches of Christ in the United States of America. Used by permission. All rights reserved.

The quotation on the back cover is from C. S. Lewis, *An Experiment in Criticism* (Cambridge: Cambridge University Press, 1961), 140–41.

ISBN: 978-1-59638-723-2 (pbk)
ISBN: 978-1-59638-724-9 (ePub)
ISBN: 978-1-59638-725-6 (Mobi)

Printed in the United States of America

Library of Congress Control Number: 2014935804

Many years ago, when I was a new Christian in a fundamentalist church, a friend newly converted from the hippie life told me that he had decided not to read anything but the Bible. I had recently become an English major at a Christian liberal arts college, and I began to wonder how my friend was going to learn to read. He wasn't illiterate, but he had no sense of what I was beginning to learn—how to understand metaphor, symbolism, and literary tone, and how to tell the literal from the literary and the straightforward from the ironic. Not that a new Christian shouldn't spend a lot of time reading the Bible, but the Bible is significantly a literary work—poetry and stories, largely—and we can better understand literature (which itself is a part of nearly all cultures) if we read and study literature. God could have chosen to reveal himself to the human race in any sort of genre he wished—essays, arguments, or letters, for example—and he did use these forms. But he often chose to reveal himself to human beings in the nearly universal art forms of poetry and story because of these forms' ability to bring meaning and significance to human life in unique ways. Studying literature, like studying any part of human culture, brings us into contact with fallen human nature, but because the literary is so central to what makes us human beings created in the image of God, studying literature is also of critical value to Christians.

WORDS AND IMAGES

Language is the fundamental building block of human consciousness and culture. The God who created human beings in his image in Genesis 1 had just called the rest of creation into being with words and had expressed in words his appreciation of the goodness of that creation, so if we ask what that divine image includes, language must be central to it. One of the first jobs assigned to Adam was to name the animals. As an analytical medium, words can organize our statements about reality and can clarify the significance of our perceptions and reactions. Visual images, such as paintings and photographs, can convey the sensory details of our experience more exactly than words can—they can show what things look like in detail. But images cannot convey abstract concepts very well; they cannot attach clear meanings to what they describe, and neither can they group a class of perceptions, ideas, objects, or actions together. When we want to do certain things, a word may be worth a thousand pictures.[1] So, when God wanted to reveal himself to human beings within the often confusing complexity of human experience, he used literary forms—narrative and poetry—to make that revelation clear.

The abstract and analytical power of language—the ability of words to convey a complex meaning through denotation and connotation—can define the meaning of an experience or mold events into a pleasing and significant order. Therefore, storytelling is one of the primary ways in which human beings communicate their sense of what

1. I don't intend to denigrate the power of film in these statements, but simply to contrast its power with that of written literature. The hackneyed criticism that film handicaps the imagination because it gives us concrete images ignores those powers of judgment and analysis that film calls us to employ. Film can convey ideas, often through specific cinematic techniques like montage and juxtaposition. And film contains language in its audio track. But the ambiguity of images is often a strength of realistic film. The meaning we derive from film must often be a product of our own analysis. Often our understanding of a film must be developed in dialog with others. The qualities of judgment we bring to film are like those we must bring to life itself. Language, on the other hand, conveys significance much more clearly. Both media have their strengths; comparing them in order to praise one over the other can be like comparing a Ferrari and a racing bicycle. The experience of using these machines is quite different, but both are amazing machines that demand our appreciation.

happens and what life is like. This principle holds both for fictional storytelling and for historical storytelling: the Greeks had a muse for history as well as a muse for epic poetry. What's important about a story is often more a matter of truth than of fact. Therefore, studying the mechanisms of storytelling, even of fictional storytelling, can help us to better understand the stories of Scripture—how they work and what they say.

Also, language, unlike realistic painting or photography, translates experience into a code that differs from what it communicates.[2] This allows for a second order of beauty, meaning, and creativity—the rhythm and sound of language, spoken or read. In poetry, this second-order code is accentuated and valued for its own sake—the sounds of words, along with their meanings, become significant in poetry. Style is a part of narrative as well. Linguistic subtlety and ingenuity are not merely an ornament of prose; they augment meaning, drawing connections between words and ideas. But in poetry, these secondary elements of language can become primary. The meanings of words explode; words become meaning-*full*. In literature, the beauty of language can be brought to the foreground. But rarely does language, even the language of poetry, escape totally from meaning. Even in an objectivist poem like William Carlos Williams's (1883–1963) "The Red Wheelbarrow," a statement is being made—the importance of the object is being asserted. In biblical poetry the message is always primary, but often the beauty of the poetic statement is part of that message—it empowers the emotion conveyed in the language, or the linguistic intensity of the statement mirrors the beauty,

---

2. I don't mean to imply that there are no codes in painting or photography, but these codes do not involve a significantly different medium; photography employs what James Monaco calls "a short-circuit sign, in which signifier and signified are nearly the same" (*How to Read a Film*, 4th ed. [Oxford: Oxford University Press, 2009]: 176). Language and what it points to are vastly different things.

profundity, or even the horror of the statement being made. How could the Creator of wildflowers and woodlands not reveal himself in a beautiful way?

Words and The Word

The beauty of biblical literature is a product of the talents of great writers working within the literary traditions of their cultures. We shouldn't let our emphasis on the inspiration and infallibility of Scripture blind us to the human, literary character of God's revelation of himself. Because I had put the Bible in a separate category from the rest of literature, I defended the calling to become a writer of imaginative literature to Christian students for decades before I realized that the Bible is obviously a defense of literature and writing in itself. Wanting to reveal himself to the human race, God employed the talents of some of the greatest writers of prose and poetry in human history: Isaiah, Jeremiah, Luke, the authors of Job and Hebrews, Hannah, the Virgin Mary, David, and the other Psalmists, not to mention the writers of the historical narratives in Genesis, Judges, Ruth, Samuel, Kings, and Chronicles, whether those were individuals or generations of storytellers. God used the literary traditions of Hebrew culture as a vehicle for his revelation of himself to the human race. And while some of the particular techniques of Hebrew poetry and storytelling may differ from those of our own literature, the differences are not a difference in kind. Understanding the literature of our culture and other cultures can help us to understand the literature of Scripture, which we must understand in order to understand the message of God's revelation.

THE PLEASURES OF THE TEXT

Therefore, if we want to understand God's revelation fully, we Christians need to understand the literary forms that it comes in. But these reasons for studying literature aren't sufficient. Literature would be, according to these arguments, merely a secular means to a spiritual end; it would be an interesting elective course for Bible majors. We would put up with studying literature in order to get to what is really profitable—the study of Scripture; we would mine literature for examples of literary techniques that would illuminate what the Bible is doing or would turn to literature when we were stumped about the Psalms or Lamentations. But literature is a joy in its own right as well. If that were not so, why would people throughout human history have dedicated so much of their time to reading and writing it? One of the reasons that God revealed himself in poetry and stories is that he wanted us to enjoy his revelation.

Of course, though, not all joys are a benefit to us. I'll refrain from listing here the myriad "joyous" activities that beckon to us in our contemporary world and would lead us into sin and misery. I suspect that my friend who had decided to read nothing but the Bible was fearful of giving himself over to one of these sorts of sinful joys. Many people see literature this way; they fear being drawn emotionally into sympathizing with a sinful character or being seduced by the dramatic logic of a pernicious author. This is, of course, a real danger. The literary talent of the sorts of writers who have made it into the canons of college English departments makes the force of their writing even more dangerous for young readers. But I have always argued that the biblical solution to this difficulty is not withdrawing from culture, but rather learning how to read wisely and perceptively. The apostle Paul argues in Ephesians that sin itself can be a bearer of the light if it is clearly exposed.

> Have nothing to do with the fruitless deeds of darkness, but rather expose them. It is shameful even to mention

what the disobedient do in secret. But everything exposed by the light becomes visible—and everything that is illuminated becomes a light. (Eph. 5:11–14).

When we, as Christians, learn to analyze literary works, we may be freed from being manipulated by powerful writers. When we shine the light of our Christian understanding on what we read, it illuminates the nature of the work and the purpose of its author. This sort of analytical skill can benefit us in every area of life, especially in our involvement with other art forms like film and music. Christians need to grow up and get involved, and at the same time need to go from being mindless consumers to being thoughtful analysts and critics.

Flannery O'Connor (1925–1964) was a card-carrying member of the guild of modern fiction writers and, at the same time, a devout Catholic. She understood the sorts of demands that modern fiction placed upon its readers. Responding to a controversy over what was being taught in the high school curriculum of the state of Georgia in 1963, she wrote this:

> The high school English teacher will be fulfilling his responsibility if he furnishes the student a guided opportunity through the best writing of the past, to come, in time, to an understanding of the best writing of the present. . . .
>
> And if the student finds that this is not to his taste? Well, that is regrettable. His taste should not be consulted; it is being formed.[3]

O'Connor acknowledged the moral danger in the sort of fiction that she herself wrote—modern fiction that involves the reader in the sinful actions and feelings of characters—

3. "Fiction Is a Subject with a History—It Should Be Taught That Way," in *Collected Works* (New York: Library of America, 1988), 852.

but the antidote she recommended is the development of taste and critical ability through a chronological study of English and American literature.

So it is important that we develop a sort of split personality in our reading. We need, on the one hand, to be open to the text—to allow it to do to us what the writer intended and to stir our feelings, emotions, and imagination. We need to consider the experiences and ideas being presented to us. But, on the other hand, we need to develop our ability to hover above our own reading selves, watching, judging, and critiquing. It is certainly right for us to enter into "the pleasures of the text." Language is a gift of God, as is the skill of those who can use it well. On the other hand, all human products have been tainted by the fall, and part of learning to live as Christians in this world is to develop an ability to sort through our experiences and to judge them. Certainly, we can also become so enamored with art that we neglect our duty to live in reality, and that sort of addiction needs to be avoided. But these aren't good reasons to avoid literature entirely any more than fear of gluttony is a justification for anorexia.

In studying literature we explore another part of God's creation, and deepening our understanding of God's natural and human creation deepens our sense of wonder and appreciation before the Creator of its order, beauty, and significance. God created a beautiful world, and he gave us the ability to intuit, understand, imitate, appreciate, and enjoy that beauty.[4] So human beings have always delighted in fashioning beautiful things out of the raw material that God created. Language is one of these raw materials we have always delighted in using.

---

4. When I speak of beauty I don't mean to limit art to the portrayal of pleasant, attractive things. I am referring to the skillful or pleasing form or mode of expression that is used in creating a work of art.

In the last few decades of his life, my father took up woodcarving as a hobby. For years I watched him whittle away at blocks of pine, creating forms that had a pleasing shape. When I began to write seriously in college, I came to think of what I was doing as the same sort of thing; woodcarving became an illuminating metaphor for me. Our human sense of beauty and order is linked to what we see in our heavenly Father's creation. Our ancestors have whittled away at words, and the form and detail of their stories, essays, or poems, like the form of atoms and molecules, can fill us with wonder and pleasure as we learn to appreciate and understand it.

So studying literature, like studying any of the fine arts, means learning to understand and appreciate beautiful objects of a certain sort. What sorts of objects are literary works? Stories are like paintings in that they create a picture of reality, but they also move through time like drama and music. A story or poem is an ordering of words like the ordering of notes. Poems have always been called songs because poetry is composed of beautiful sounds recited over a period of time. The written representation is more important in poetry than in song, however, because poems get written down and placed on a page. Music can also be sheet music, but sheet music is intended for performance, not to be read silently. Also, poetry is an ordering not only of sounds but also of images and ideas. Poems paint pictures, but unlike paintings and music they paint with words, which are symbols to which we have attached meanings. In the best of poems, meaning and form are mated together perfectly. What is said can be said only in the way it is being said.

A BEAUTIFUL "DESIGN"

For example, consider Robert Frost's (1874–1963) sonnet "Design." I've chosen this poem because I find it beautiful and fascinating and because it is an accessible poem by one of the most accessible of American poets. As is true of most Frost poems, however, a profound significance lies beneath its simple surface; it addresses an idea that is familiar to most Christians and points out questions we need to pay attention to.

Design

I found a dimpled spider, fat and white,
On a white heal-all, holding up a moth
Like a white piece of rigid satin cloth—
Assorted characters of death and blight
Mixed ready to begin the morning right,
Like the ingredients of a witches' broth—
A snow-drop spider, a flower like a froth,
And dead wings carried like a paper kite.

What had that flower to do with being white,
The wayside blue and innocent heal-all?
What brought the kindred spider to that height,
Then steered the white moth thither in the night?
What but design of darkness to appall?—
If design govern in a thing so small.[5]

The title of the poem can be read in a number of ways. The poet finds an intricate and beautiful arrangement of natural things: a white spider on top of a white flower holding the body of a white moth. He calls it a "snow-drop spider" because the white spider's eight symmetrical legs remind him of the six symmetrical points of a snowflake. The white-on-white "design" seems beautiful to him—a natural design. But the word *design* also reminds us of the theological "argument from design." If you, like me, grew up

5. Robert Frost, "Design," in *American Poetry, 1922: A Miscellany* (New York: Harcourt, Brace, and Company, 1922), 38.

on Moody Science films, or if you've been paying attention to recent arguments about "intelligent design," you know the argument well. When we look at the intricate design in the natural world, it speaks to us of the existence of its Creator. A million monkeys typing randomly on a million typewriters will not come up with Shakespeare's plays; if we find a watch lying on the ground, we know that there is, somewhere, a watchmaker. Design implies a designer. Thus, the speaker mentions the snow-drop—a common example of beautiful design at the microscopic level.

Beyond this, *design* can also be seen as a verb. Someone designs to show us something, to "steer" us toward those incidents and experiences that will mold our lives according to his will. So who or "what," as the poem asks, is this designer?

The voice of the poet in "Design" is ambivalent, shifting from wonder and admiration to sarcasm or even despair as he notices the abstract beauty of the image before him and then its deadliness. The spider is "dimpled" and the flower "like a froth" on a morning drink, but the ingredients of the "design" spell out "death and blight" and make up "a witches' broth." Even the bleak final line of the octave[6] combines a deadly synecdoche, "dead wings," with a childlike simile, "carried like a paper kite." This ambivalence feeds into the questions of the sestet.

The speaker of the poem first questions the whiteness of the image. The heal-all is usually blue, but this heal-all is sick and has turned white. Frost was an early admirer of Melville's fiction, and he often uses the color white in ways that are reminiscent of Herman Melville's (1819–1891) discussion of the color in the chapter "The Whiteness of the Whale" in *Moby-Dick*. There Melville's narrator, trying to

---

6. An octave is an eight-line stanza. In most sonnets the octave, the first eight lines, is divided from the sestet, the last six lines.

convince us that white is the most terrifying of colors, frets over the possibility that all meaning is a mere projection of the human imagination onto a world that is ultimately meaningless:

> Or is it, that as in essence whiteness is not so much a color as the visible absence of color, and at the same time the concrete of all colors; is it for these reasons that there is such a dumb blankness, full of meaning, in a wide landscape of snows—a colorless, all-color of atheism from which we shrink? . . . Nature absolutely paints like the harlot, whose allurements cover nothing but the charnel-house within. . . . And of all these things the Albino whale was the symbol.[7]

Similarly, in Frost's poem "Desert Places," the negative counterpart to the almost greeting-card image of "Stopping By Woods on a Snowy Evening," Frost paints a bleak and deadly picture of the emptiness of a snowfall on a winter landscape.[8] What scares the poet about the color white is the suggestion that, for all its beauty, nature might be empty, meaningless. The "blanker whiteness" of the snowfall is reminiscent of Melville's white whale, which suggests that behind nature there is no meaning at all, or a malevolent inhuman colossus of hatred.

"Design" suggests the possibility of a malevolent design or of no design; it seems to deny any third alternative. The whiteness of the flower and spider are ironic—they certainly don't suggest righteousness. The name "heal-all" is ironic as well; the only panacea here is death. So in the final lines the poet asks what sort of designer would create this

---

7. Herman Melville, *Moby-Dick* (New York: Harper & Brothers, 1851), 216–17.

8. Robert Frost, *A Further Range* (New York: Henry Holt, 1936), 48. The poem cannot be reproduced here because of copyright restrictions, but its text can be found online. The middle two stanzas are the most pertinent to this discussion.

beautiful horror. The word "brought" in the eleventh line becomes "steered" in the twelfth. There is no way out of the dilemma the poet constructs: if we say that design implies a designer, then we must concede that that designer controls the atrocities as well as the glories of the world. The final modulation of the speaker's voice in the last line does offer us a partial retreat. We could, perhaps, retain our belief in a general design without extending it to the minor details of the creation. But I don't think Frost takes this concession seriously. After all, Jesus himself said that a sparrow doesn't fall to the earth outside of the will of God and that the hairs of our heads are all numbered (Matt. 10:29–31). The final line of the poem simply registers the speaker's unwillingness to face the consequences of his own perception of design. Frost is helping us to feel the grim reality of our philosophical problem. He has constructed an image that links two theological ideas—the argument from design and the problem of pain. As we look out at the natural world, we see both things intimately connected.

"Design" is a sonnet, certainly one of the most beautiful and demanding forms in English poetry. A sonnet has a certain sort of perfection about it. In that way, the form of "Design" is mated to its subject. Here, too, is a thing of great beauty that in its final import is also frightening. Frost wants us to admire the beauty of his sonnet, but he expects that the more perceptive reader will sense the confusion and terror behind that beauty. Frost wrote poetry in traditional forms because he saw form as reassuring in the meaningless world of modernity. For Frost, poetic form was an example of the human attempt to give meaning and shape to the often formless and troubling events of our lives. This is frequently demonstrated in his poetry. In this poem, that beautiful form is almost ironic in the painful doubt that it expresses.

I know, of course, that there are answers to the questions that the poem raises. I see the natural world as a reflection of both the beauty of creation and the horror of the fall. To me, an image like the one in the poem reinforces my conviction that the world was in its creation "very good," yet was marred in the fall. Yet I find the poem more useful and profound than any philosophical presentation of the problem of pain. For one thing, it is simply more beautiful and delightful, despite my disagreement with its message. The voice of the poem is engaging and interesting. Frost was a poetic innovator in his use of the simple colloquial voice in his quite traditional verse. It is as though the most beautiful poetry were in hiding beneath the voice of a "plain-speaking man," a phrase often used to describe Frost's persona. The poem is also dramatic. I can feel in this poem the emotional tragedy of doubt and despair in ways that an argument can never portray. All of that is certainly worth experiencing.

A WILD PARTY

Stories, like poems, are also verbal performances; though prose, unlike music, attempts to give us some sense of the real world or of some other world that is like the real world. Fictional storytelling is mimetic, in that it tries to convey a sense of the reality of experience. Nevertheless, some writers, like Faulkner, write prose fiction that is very close to the poetic. Consider, for example, this passage from F. Scott Fitzgerald's (1896–1940) *The Great Gatsby*. It is part of a longer passage, a description of one of Gatsby's parties that introduces Fitzgerald's description of the first party that Nick Caraway attends.

> The lights grow brighter as the earth lurches away from the sun, and now the orchestra is playing yellow cocktail

music, and the opera of voices pitches a key higher. Laughter is easier minute by minute, spilled with prodigality, tipped out at a cheerful word. The groups change more swiftly, swell with new arrivals, dissolve and form in the same breath; already there are wanderers, confident girls who weave here and there among the stouter and more stable, become for a sharp, joyous moment the center of a group, and then, excited with triumph, glide on through the sea-change of faces and voices and color under the constantly changing light.

Suddenly one of the gypsies, in trembling opal, seizes a cocktail out of the air, dumps it down for courage and, moving her hands like Frisco, dances out alone on the canvas platform. A momentary hush; the orchestra leader varies his rhythm obligingly for her, and there is a burst of chatter as the erroneous news goes around that she is Gilda Grey's understudy from the *Follies*. The party has begun.[9]

Every time I read this passage I am surprised and amazed by the last sentence. Fitzgerald has an infallible sense of pacing and of tone here. He is describing a joyous occasion, but more than that he is trying to help us to feel an intoxicating excitement that is cultural, emotional, even physical. So he pushes his language up to the borders of what is possible in prose. He uses a technique called synesthesia, a blurring of the senses. It's what John Keats does in his "Ode to a Nightingale"[10] and "Ode on a Grecian Urn,"[11] in which he hears the image of a piper or drinks sunshine and poetry; or like Emily Dickinson's describing the "blue, uncertain stumbling buzz"[12] of the fly heard at the moment

9. F. Scott Fitzgerald, *The Great Gatsby* (New York: Charles Scribner's Sons, 1925; repr. New York: Scribner, 2004), 40–41.
10. Quoted in Margaret Ferguson, Mary Jo Salter, and Jon Stallworthy, *The Norton Anthology of Poetry, Shorter Fourth Edition* (New York: W. W. Norton & Company, 1997), 509–11.
11. Quoted in ibid., 512–13.
12. Quoted in ibid., 634–35.

of death. Fitzgerald points out the "yellow cocktail music" and the laughter like spilled drinks. His metaphors are complex and multifaceted. Take that spilled laughter, for example. It is Prohibition—liquor is expensive and hard to get. In the same way, laughter and happiness are precious commodities. But at this party they are concentrated into delicious excess, so much so that they are being spilled out onto the grass. The word "prodigal" denotes careless excess, though it also has a biblical ring that reminds us of the eventual end of excess. And the spilling reminds us of the ritual of libation, pouring out wine for the gods to drink.

Gatsby's party is cosmic in its proportions. The sun doesn't set; rather, "the earth lurches away" from it. And when the earth does that, rather than darkness setting in, the lighting grows even brighter against the dark backdrop. The party is a work of art, an "opera of voices"; it is a physical phenomenon as groups form and dissolve and form once again like molecules in suspension. And the epitome of the party's magic is seen in the behavior of the bold young woman who confidently expresses its abandon in her dance after magically "seizing" a cocktail "out of the air." The rhythm and cadence and breathless poetry of Fitzgerald's sentences augment the power of his description. Then, in the final sentence, he stops, steps back, and states the simple fact. Following the longer, more complicated sentences with the short, simple, frank, four-word statement increases the emotional power of those four words. And the irony of the word "begun" turns all the poetic enthusiasm of the paragraph into a multiplier of something even more exciting to come. Fitzgerald has given us a sense of the emotional power of this symbolic moment of jazz-age gaiety.

But, of course, what Fitzgerald is describing is also immoral and illegal. Earlier in the passage he tells us that the party is composed of "men and girls"[13]; he tells us that the bar is stocked with exotic liquors "so long forgotten that most of [the] *female* guests were too young to know one from another."[14] Later he will say that "while church bells rang out along shore, the world and its mistress twinkled hilariously on [Gatsby's] lawn."[15] It's important at this point in the novel that we sense the jazz-age excitement of Gatsby's parties and the enthusiasm and "romantic readiness" of his "heightened sensitivity to the promise of life,"[16] but if we also catch a note of hubris, that this cannot go on forever, we are on to something. Later, Gatsby's attempt to reconstruct the romantic promise of his past will founder on the rocks of his own corruption, the insubstantiality of its object—Daisy Buchanan—and the reality of the emptiness of the modern wasteland. However, the greatness of Fitzgerald's art has always seemed to me to be his ability to combine the romantic hopes and dreams of the American past with the emptiness and moral bankruptcy of the modern world of naturalism. So, at the end of the novel, he reminds us of the Dutch sailors' first glimpse of the "fresh green breast" of the new world and of their "capacity for wonder."[17] All of the force of this romantic desire for hope and joy, so well dramatized throughout the novel, stands behind this wonderful description of Gatsby's parties.

I could certainly provide multiple passages from Fitzgerald's masterpiece to demonstrate the joys of fiction—and I could point to Faulkner, Hawthorne, Melville, and many other American authors who were able to marshal the power of words to create complicated effects in prose passages like this one. But this passage will need to suffice.

13. Fitzgerald, *The Great Gatsby*, 39.
14. Ibid., 40.
15. Ibid., 61.
16. Ibid., 2.
17. Ibid., 182.

A JOB DONE WELL

It's hard to identify and define all the pleasures that literary works of this sort provide. There is, of course, the joy of seeing something done well—the sort of joy we get when we see any excellent performance. It is delightful to see human talent at its best. But, particularly when we read poetry, the words on the page and in the ear are delightful as well. If one reads enough sonnets, one gets used to the form. The sonnet becomes a familiar object, a recognizable shape. It is a frame of a standard size. Seeing someone fill that container well and do something delightful with that set form is even more delightful for the aficionado—the reader of Shakespeare's, Milton's, and Wordsworth's sonnets. There is also the delight of well-made phrases like "design of darkness" and "dimpled spider, fat and white." The beauty of "Design" makes it seem inevitable, a little piece of perfection. This had to be said in this way. This sonnet needed to be just the way it is; no word is out of place. Furthermore, the voice of the poem is easy, natural, and colloquial. The poetic is contained in the everyday, and it's delightful to find out the inner beauty.

The same things can be said for beautiful prose. It too has a rhythm and a sound. Stories also delight us in ways that are more familiar but equally mysterious. We enjoy entering the experience of others through the spoken or written word. We enjoy having human experience presented in a way that is formed and organized; the form of a plot, like the form of a poem, comforts us in a world that can seem formless. Writers bring to stories their own experiences, their recommendations about meaning. And when the story is well told, when the voice of the storyteller is beautiful and evocative, it draws us away from our own range of experiences into a more intriguing account of human life.

Of course, not all stories are happy ones, and many people don't enjoy reading tragedies. But the fact that some people do is mysterious. I've always wondered why satisfying stories, even if they are happy, always involve some sort of conflict, a threat overcome, a resolution of tension. Pure, untempered happiness never makes for a good story. Why is that? Does it mean that literature panders to our fallen nature? I don't think so. The appeal of conflict is simply a reflection of the human condition. The first human story is of a man who is alone and finds a partner; the second is of their fall. Perhaps we will develop a different sort of storytelling in the new age, but right now we are stuck with the human condition. So Aristotle says that tragedy purges us through pity and fear, and that we enjoy that catharsis[18]—as good a theory as any. When we read narrative, we delight in the beauty of the form and the beauty of the telling, even if we regret what the characters do or what happens to them and empathize with their experience.

I think literature does something else for us as well—it gives us what I've come to think of as inner resources. The presence of the Holy Spirit in our lives, our fellowship with God, is our greatest inner resource. However, a mind stocked with beautiful language, great examples of human art, also has resources to call upon in lonely or troubling times—memories beyond our own, the experiences of other people. Sometimes people avoid English classes and major in business or computer science because they want to become rich and they believe that those majors will get them a better job. But there are types of riches that can't be reduced to dollars and cents—how sad to have a well-furnished apartment but a mind that can't remember (or has never encountered) the beautiful forms and profound expressions of our cultural tradition.

18. Aristotle, "Poetics," *The Complete Works of Aristotle*, trans. Jonathan Barnes (Oxford: Oxford University Press, 1984), 2320.

SINGING SCHOOL

Beyond delighting us through their beauty, great works of literature can serve as models for us in our own attempts to use the English language well. In his poem "Sailing to Byzantium," the Irish poet W. B. Yeats (1865–1939), seeking a sort of immortality in meditation on Byzantine art, writes,

> An aged man is but a paltry thing,
> A tattered coat upon a stick, unless
> Soul clap its hands and sing, and louder sing
> For every tatter in its mortal dress,
> Nor is there singing school but studying
> Monuments of its own magnificence.[19]

We learn how to write by studying good, even great, writing. This needn't involve the sort of direct imitation that used to be a staple of English instruction, but experiencing the effect that the work of accomplished writers has on us can show us the capabilities of language and can help us to learn how to achieve the sorts of effects we want to achieve.

When I write fiction, I can't help but write the sort of fiction I read. Unfortunately for me, I've read quite a bit of nineteenth-century American fiction. Nathaniel Hawthorne (1804–1864) refined and perfected a writing style that came to him from the great English writers of the seventeenth century, through Washington Irving and James Fenimore Cooper. His prose is masterful and amazing. As an example, consider this passage, a favorite of mine—in which Hawthorne's narrator is elaborating on his fictitious claim to have gotten the story behind *The Scarlet Letter* from a historical manuscript composed by the dead former customs inspector Jonathan Pew:

---

19. Quoted in Ferguson, Salter, and Stallworthy, *The Norton Anthology of Poetry*, 681–82.

> I must not be understood as affirming, that, in the dressing up of the tale, and imagining the motives and modes of passion that influenced the characters who figure in it, I have invariably confined myself within the limits of the old Surveyor's half a dozen sheets of foolscap. On the contrary, I have allowed myself, as to such points, nearly or altogether as much license as if the facts had been entirely of my own invention. What I contend for is the authenticity of the outline.[20]

These three sentences are like a tangled piece of string that unravels in our hands and then disappears. The complicated qualifications of the second sentence—a positive sentence balanced against the negative first sentence—end up undoing any of the claims to historical fact made earlier. When Josef Sommer, playing Customs Inspector Hawthorne in the prologue to the PBS *Scarlet Letter* miniseries in 1979, speaks these lines, he pauses, turns to the audience with a thoughtful look, and sets off the "or altogether" ironically. I think this emphasis is right. If a writer takes altogether as much liberty with the facts as he would if he invented them himself, he is admitting that he invented them himself. The final sentence makes a claim for the fictional authenticity of the book as a historical romance, which will illuminate our understanding of seventeenth-century New England and therefore of Hawthorne's nineteenth-century New England.

Woe to the modern writer who tries to publish a sentence like that one! But the wit, irony, and intelligence of Hawthorne's style can certainly be translated into modern prose. I've had to struggle to shorten my sentences and write more straightforwardly, but I think I've caught something good from steeping myself in Hawthorne and Melville.

20. Nathaniel Hawthorne, *The Scarlet Letter* (Boston: Ticknor, Reed, and Fields, 1850; repr. London: Knight and Son, 1851), 43.

Another set of American writers is more directly translatable into our struggles to communicate in twenty-first century America. After the Romantic period, American writers developed a much less ornate prose style. An important influence in developing this style was the newspaper. Many of our greatest writers served a sort of apprenticeship in journalism, which helped to put them in touch with the popular audience and taught them to write more simply and clearly. I don't mean by commending these writers to disparage the work of writers like Melville and Faulkner. But just as painters need art school training in sketching, most of us need to master simple and direct prose before we move toward the poetic.

Walt Whitman (1819–1892) is recognized as the most American of American poets because of both the form and the subjects of his poetry. He turned from conventional meter to the rhythms of oratory and argument and the King James Bible. He turned from rhyme to a broader sense of the music and beauty of language. "America is herself the greatest poem," Whitman says in his preface to *Leaves of Grass*.[21] Whitman modeled the form of his poetry after the form of the American republic—many states forming a united whole, people of many different sorts becoming united into a democratic order in diversity. That Whitman conceives of his poems in this way explains why he so often uses the catalog,[22] calling forth diverse people, objects, and experiences to stand together in the unity of his poetic structures. The greatest example of this is "Song of Myself,"[23] an enormous poem whose poetic and philosophical structure can contain everything Walt Whitman has seen and known

21. "Preface," *Whitman: Poetry and Prose* (New York: Library of America, 1982), 5.

22. The catalog, a long list of characters or objects, is a poetic technique dating back to Homer's epics. Homer listed soldiers or boats or horses; Whitman often lists diverse inhabitants of Manhattan or of the American states.

23. Walt Whitman, "Song of Myself," in *Leaves of Grass* (Philadelphia: Sherman & Co., 1883), 31–79.

as well as what he has read—the experiences of men and of women, of slave and of free, of high and of low, all united by the democratic voice of the American poet, by the sympathy and understanding of the poet who loves and embraces them all as part of the great poem that is America itself. What we can learn from Whitman is the value of close factual observation—what Whitman learned as a reporter. Whitman also demonstrates the power of simple words; he believed that naming a person or thing called that thing into being in the mind of his reader.

I find the same sort of simple power in the poetry of William Carlos Williams (1883–1963), who was very much influenced by Whitman as well as by the literary modernists of the Imagist movement.[24] Williams, too, believed in the power of simple words. As a pediatrician, he learned to observe people exactly and to use language concisely. Here, for example, is part of his description of the plants he sees "on the road to the contagious hospital" from his poem "Spring and All":

> They enter the new world naked,
> cold, uncertain of all
> save that they enter. All about them
> the cold, familiar wind—
>
> Now the grass, tomorrow
> the stiff curl of wildcarrot leaf
>
> One by one objects are defined—
> It quickens: clarity, outline of leaf

24. *Imagism* was a poetic movement of the early twentieth century that stressed the importance of an image rather than a thematic statement in poetry. The image could be a vivid picture of an object or an abstract shape or pattern, but it could also be a tone of voice or a frame of mind. Ezra Pound (1885–1973) and Hilda Doolittle (1886–1961) were the two most significant American adherents to the original movement.

But now the stark dignity of
entrance—Still, the profound change
has come upon them: rooted they
grip down and begin to awaken[25]

Williams strains to grab a hold of the exact moment when spring enters the world, as if it were the moment when Hades releases Persephone into the upper world or the moment of a child's birth. In writing the poem, Williams assists in the birth of the new season—he calls the moment into being. Williams was an "objectivist"—he saw poems as brand new artistic objects and carefully typed them out, experimenting with shapes and forms on the page. I don't intend to recommend Williams' aesthetic theory so much as to point out that it bred a concise simplicity in his poetry that we would do well to imitate.

A third writer who is instructive in this regard is Ernest Hemingway (1899–1961), an author who labored hard to develop the simplicity of his prose. According to a display at the Hemingway Museum in his hometown of Oak Park, Illinois, Hemingway, when telegraphing his dispatches from Europe as a reporter for the *Kansas City Star*, learned how to eliminate all unnecessary words from his prose. He called the quality that this gave his prose "the power of omission." Hemingway believed that, even if a writer didn't reveal all that he knew about a situation or his characters, these omitted details would still be present for the reader. It was important for the writer to be aware of these omitted details, but he needn't describe them. Hemingway always said that he wrote on what he called the iceberg principle—that only one eighth of the iceberg is visible above the water, but the seven eighths

25. By William Carlos Williams, from *The Collected Poems: Volume I, 1909–1939*, copyright © 1938 by New Directions Publishing Corp. Reprinted by permission of New Directions Publishing Corp.

below the surface is what moves the iceberg and gives it its force. Hemingway's style is unmistakable and the power of his simple prose is profound.

These American writers are good models of prose and poetry for aspiring students; their literary techniques are worth studying and striving to understand. However, contemporary prose often strays from these good models.

A CATALOG OF CONTEMPORARY SINS

One of my struggles with freshmen in composition class is to get them to observe details. I can't count how many times I've received an essay about growing up and asked in my comments, "But what did your boyfriend look like?" or "What was the color and make of this car that signaled the beginning of your manhood?" Often the ambiguity of these students' essays is caused by their choice of vague words. They learn to "deal with" the "issues" that have "impacted them" or "blown them away." But what does "deal with" mean? Does it mean to ignore? To learn from? To accept? Are they suffering from depression (or merely sadness), depravity, disgust, or dysentery?

My students also seem to think, as Jesus put it, "that they will be heard because of their many words" (Matt. 6:7 NRSV). They like wordy formulas: "at the hour of ten o'clock p.m. in the evening" rather than "at ten p.m."; "I am generally supportive of" rather than "I support." They like the sound of big words, words like "utilize," "situate," or "intentionality," rather than "use," "put," or "purpose." I know where they have caught this disease—it is everywhere around them in the culture. We speak in clichés and let common, worn-out phrases do our thinking for us. Too often the discourse my students hear in the college classroom is dense and jargon-laden, and they get the impression that such language is powerful and respected, the mark of education and sophistication. But the purpose of writing and speaking, I tell them, is to communicate, not to show off.

Furthermore, clichés derail the process of thought. They make it easier to deceive ourselves about the meaning of what we are saying. The greatest study of the effect of these poor habits on modern thought is George Orwell's (1903–1950) "Politics and the English Language,"[26] in which Orwell lays out the sins of modern prose and shows how they blind us to reality. Phrases like "revenue enhancements" (taxes), "illegal deprivation of life" (political murder), and "radiation enhancement weapon" (the neutron bomb) hide the reality of our decisions and deceive our listeners. When I heard a military commander say in a news interview, "Our thoughts and prayers is with them" [*sic*], I realized that "thoughts and prayers" had become a meaningless cliché used mainly by people who don't pray at all and try hard not to think. (By the way, people usually say this about the relatives of people who have "passed" or "passed on" or "passed away." No one is so crass as to *die* anymore—not even literary characters.)

Sadly, these same sorts of linguistic diseases have infected the church. Christians should study great literature because many of them will be called to be writers someday, some even to preach the gospel within our culture. Many preachers don't know how to write a good essay, so how can they preach a good sermon? My students, who respect their pastors, try to copy their pastors' ways of speaking. They "are mindful of" things; they "have a heart for" all sorts of things—for everything, it seems, except pumping blood. And it's no wonder that their hearts can't pump blood; God is always "laying things" on their hearts. They look at life "relationally," they "engage the culture," and they are "cognizant" of things. I suspect that our inability

26. *George Orwell: A Collection of Essays* (New York: Harcourt, 1981), 156–70.

to understand the nature of our spiritual lives is a function of the vague ways in which we allow ourselves to describe them. If we regret that so many talented writers have aligned themselves against the church and have used their literary powers to serve our enemy, we should fight back by developing our powers and putting them in service to God. The apostle Paul says in 1 Corinthians 2:12–13 that the Holy Spirit helps us to find the words to share with others what God has given us. But few Christian writers and speakers rise above the clichés of our culture or of the church; few of them seem to care about the state of the language that God, in his providence, has given them to use.

LITERATURE AND CONTEMPORARY ARTS

Of course, many people would concede that literary study has all the value I have attributed to it and yet would never read the great literary works of our culture unless they were forced to by an English teacher like me. In our day storytelling and poetry have waned, largely because more technologically advanced forms of art have absorbed them. Storytelling has given way to moviemaking, and poetry has given way to song. In our culture, the older art forms exist now largely as preparation for the newer forms: novels are prototypes of movies, and poems are lyrics waiting for a tune. But the older art forms have an integrity of their own that has been limited and lost sight of in the current situation, and they have a power that differs from the power of the newer forms that have replaced them. I have never thought of the rise of film and of popular music as a sign of the end of the age or a symptom of social decay; I have enjoyed the glories of film and song too much to condemn them. But I do think that it is important to preserve our cultural heritage by understanding the older art forms. Verbal art and visual art are different from literary art.

We perceive them differently and they involve different ways of thinking. An educated person must develop the mental processes fostered by both sorts of art. Also, those who want to express themselves in the newer recorded arts would do well to serve an apprenticeship in the older arts. Cinema begins with literature, in the screenplay, and ends with literature, in analysis and criticism.

Most films begin as written text whether or not they are adapted from novels. Words help us to understand and analyze the images we construct in film, and obviously writing dialog bridges the two media. More than that, the origins of storytelling are in the literary realm, not in the visual realm. A former student of mine who now teaches film complains frequently of his students' inability to tell stories or even to understand what stories are and how they work. The great myths and plots of human life have come down to us in our cultures' literary traditions. All the great emotions and occasions of life have yielded poetic themes and forms.

Certainly, part of learning to live in the modern world is learning to understand images as well. Some of the greatest filmmakers, like Alfred Hitchcock (1899–1980) and Steven Spielberg (1946–), have had wonderful visual imaginations—a sense of how images speak to us and what they mean when they are connected together. So I don't mean to imply that literary study is, by itself, an adequate preparation for a career in film or even for living in the contemporary world. But both of these filmmakers have also been great storytellers. Spielberg's *E.T.* (1982) is a retelling of the Christ story, whether Spielberg admits that or not. *E.T.* and *Close Encounters of the Third Kind* (1977) were popular because people in American culture were tired of disillusionment and hopelessness. They responded joyfully to these stories of intrusions from beings outside of our mundane reality, of the arrival of miraculous strangers with the healing touch or the power to give us meaning, who die and then ascend into heaven or take us away to a greater, more wonderful place.

Hitchcock storyboarded his movies elaborately; he himself didn't write the scripts. He thought in images; he knew what would work cinematically and he chose stories that could be told well on the screen. It's interesting that Hitchcock never filmed a classic story. The closest he came to that was *Rebecca* (1940), and while directing that movie he fought constantly with David Selznick, the producer, who demanded faithfulness to the text. Hitchcock liked to pick something not well known, pull out the kernel he liked, and throw the rest of the story away. He wanted to be free to construct the twists and turns of his elaborate plots in conference with his screenwriters. Hitchcock brought his visual talent and his sense of how stories are told in cinema to the process of constructing a narrative of a certain sort—the suspense story. So these great masters of visual culture understood the significance of the literary antecedents of their works, and the importance of storytelling, even as they adapted stories and archetypes from literature to the newer art of film.

Likewise, while a folk singer like Loreena McKennitt (1957–) has been able to adapt poems of Shakespeare, Yeats, and Tennyson to Celtic melodies, most popular music does not rise to that level of literary sophistication—nor does it need to. Certainly Bob Dylan (1941–) and Bruce Cockburn (1945–) deserve to be acclaimed as contemporary poets, and it is no accident that Dylan took the last name of his stage name (he was born as Robert Zimmerman) from the name of the great Irish poet Dylan Thomas (1914–1953) who influenced him. Cockburn's lyrics are often so literary that they need to escape the confines of their musical containers, becoming more like free verse. It's interesting to me that popular music in rap and hip-hop has as much as acknowledged its ambition to become poetry.

But the lyrics of some of the best contemporary popular songs are bare and boring; they rely on the power of their musical accompaniment to succeed in nonverbal ways. Poetry, on the other hand, actually increases its power by divesting itself of music—it needs to rely solely on the musical elements in language.

Not only does literary work precede these newer arts, it follows them. We analyze, understand, and appreciate what we have seen and heard through language. Certainly one can respond to a film with film; as film became a more sophisticated medium throughout the twentieth century, filmmakers became more conscious of speaking into a medium with a canon and a tradition. But a verbal response has a different nature—only through words can we analyze, evaluate, and discuss. And these ways of understanding are even more important when we are attempting to understand non-verbal art. Images and sounds cannot convey ideas in the way that words can. In contemporary society we are called to learn to speak in both ways.

STEWARDS OF OUR LANGUAGE

Occasionally a student will come into my office and will justify a low grade or a poorly written essay by saying, "I've never liked English." My stock reply is, "Have you tried German?" I don't mean to insult the German language; it just seems ironic that someone would say he doesn't like a language that he will probably spend his whole life using constantly. If we are going to use a car, most of us feel some responsibility for its maintenance; if we are going to use the English language, we need to dedicate at least some of our time to learning to use it well. As Yeats argues in

"Sailing to Byzantium," we can do that only by studying the monuments to the language that exist in our literary tradition. When we read well-written literature, a strange sort of alchemy occurs, and we find that our leaden words are slowly transmuted into gold.

READING AND PROFITING FROM THE LITERATURE OF SCRIPTURE

At the beginning of this booklet, I mentioned a friend who had decided to read only the Bible; I said that I wondered how he would learn to read, and I suggested that reading literature can make us better readers of Scripture. Looking back over my experience as a Christian, I can see how God has used my literary study to enhance my understanding and enjoyment of the Bible.

I was raised in a fundamentalist dispensationalist church. I was taught that the Bible needs to be read literally. My teachers knew that when Jesus said, "I am the door," he didn't mean that he was made out of wood, but they believed that "Israel" always meant Israel, in an ethnic, genetic sense. Even the images of the book of Revelation they tried to take as literally as possible. Now when people (usually unbelieving skeptics) ask me if I take the Bible "literally," I tell them that I take it "literarily"—that I try to understand what sort of literature it is, and what the writer's intention is, before I interpret it.

The Bible is a literary book. Even when it is historical, God reveals himself in what the writer of Hebrews calls "shadow[s]" (Heb. 10:1) and "illustration[s]" (9:9) and "copies of . . . heavenly things" (9:23). Therefore the questions that come up when we interpret the Bible are literary questions. To read the Bible well, we need to be able to spot, understand, and interpret figures of speech. Much of this ability we gain only by acquiring a love for, and an understanding of, other great literature. Unsophisticated readers can certainly understand and appreciate Scripture; the doctrine of the perspicuity of Scripture applies to all of us. But unsophisticated readers read the Bible in an unsophisticated way. Many of the misunderstandings and misapplications that plague the church and cause needless divisions arise from these unsophisticated readings.

Reading stories has made me a better reader of the stories of Scripture. Now that my ear has been trained to hear an ironic tone, when I read the story of Gideon in Judges—truly the work of a master storyteller—I can better understand and appreciate the wonderful irony that suffuses it. Having read Oedipus the King, I now recognize that God, though not mentioned directly in Esther, speaks through the ironic justice visited on the villain Haman. I understand that the Bible often intends to provoke me to imagine an unspoken background, to ask questions that the text does not explicitly answer. Why does David, in 1 Samuel 27, go over to the side of the Philistines in despair? What does this lapse indicate about the state of his faith at that period in his life, and how does that fit into the story of his obedience and disobedience throughout his life? How does God respond to that situation? When I ask and answer these questions, I use imaginative resources that I have developed from reading the novels of Hawthorne and Dickens and George Eliot, and the stories of Scripture in turn inform me about God, human nature, and my own experience.

But beyond that, studying literature has taught me to see the Bible more clearly as a human book containing stories and poems that reflect human nature and culture as well as seeing it as a revelation of God's will and his actions in history. Before I became a student of literature, I often read the Bible as though it were a book of doctrine or systematic theology disguised as a literary text. The human element was just a wrapper to be removed and disposed of. The doctrinal content was like the kernel of a nut. Once I broke open the nut and got at its meat, the shell was worthless and could be thrown away; it had no nutritional value. When I read the Bible this way, reducing it to "propositional statements" about God or about the Christian life, the Bible became a closed book to me, the experience of reading it almost a rote recitation of passages that I already knew the meaning of. I quickly moved beyond the literary—the element of human experience—to the theological.

At best, for example, when I read the story of Abraham and Isaac, I was reminded of the duties of the Christian life, that I was to make obedience to God my ultimate goal in life, my highest priority. Abraham and Isaac became unnecessary figures in a text that was making a doctrinal statement. Though I was committed to the historical reality of the story, even that was necessary only as a prop for the doctrine of inerrancy.

But when I began to see the Bible as a work of literature, as being a human work as well as being God's revelation of himself to me, reading it became much more meaningful and personal. I saw Abraham as a father like me, and I experienced the pain of his mission. The mysterious command of God became a significant living episode in the life of a man like me. Unlike Abraham, I have the benefit of centuries of biblical revelation—I have the benefit of being able to read the story of Abraham's crisis of faith. But I, too, face the daily experience of living my life in communion with an invisible God whose ways are beyond my comprehension and often cause me to question them. Entering into the story of Abraham, empathizing with his troubling experience, and admiring his unconditional trust and obedience helps me to better understand and endure my own crises—those times when the experience of my life challenges my logical doctrinal convictions. It teaches me that having faith isn't having a consistent set of answers and holding to a set of propositions; it's trusting in a living God who is working through my struggles to make me more like his Son.

As I studied literature and began to understand how stories work, I began to understand why God chose to reveal himself to us in stories. God doesn't want to give me simply a set of ideas to believe, principles to live by, or a "world view" or frame of reference; God wants to be part of my story and wants me to be part of his story. The experience of reading the stories of the Bible is meant to be a means of grace, to enable me to better face my life emotionally and spiritually as well as intellectually.

The deficiencies of reading the Bible as a set of propositional statements and the benefits of reading it as a work of literature are compounded when we think about reading biblical poetry. The Psalms are the only poems many Christians ever read. Happily, we also sing hymns on Sundays, but the poetry of hymns is limited to certain tones of voice that the Psalms often transcend. Surely reading the great poems of our own language will help to tune our ears to hear the voices of the psalmists better. And it will help us to better express our praise, our questions, our emotional reactions, our wonder. Reading Frost's "Design" and hearing the struggles of its speaker to reconcile his encounter with death with the sovereignty of God, or reading Shakespeare's *King Lear*, sends me back to Scripture—not just to find answers, but to be better able to experience the poignant poetic accounts of biblical writers. Of course the book of Job is a source for both of these great works of literature. But other biblical texts also dramatize the problem of evil.

Psalm 73 is one of my favorites. Rather than presenting a logical argument or a philosophical answer to the question of the prosperity of the wicked, Psalm 73 recounts the emotional experience of Asaph.

But as for me, my feet had almost slipped;
   I had nearly lost my foothold.
For I envied the arrogant
   when I saw the prosperity of the wicked. (vv. 2–3)

Asaph describes the charmed life of the wicked and complains about the effect of their prosperity on the morale of others:

Therefore their people turn to them
   and drink up waters in abundance.
They say, "How would God know?
   Does the Most High know anything?" (vv. 10–11)

His poetic statement conveys to us the feelings of frustration that we, too, often feel when we see the wicked advanced and God's name treated as irrelevant. And Asaph confesses that this has affected his own attitude as well; he, too, has questioned the value of righteous behavior.

Surely in vain I have kept my heart pure
   and have washed my hands in innocence.
All day long I have been afflicted,
   and every morning brings new punishments. (vv. 13–14)

Asaph looks deeply into his own response to the experience of injustice. He will describe his repentance of these attitudes, but not before he makes them dramatic and real to us—not before he points out to God the effect of God's seeming indifference.

Like Job, Asaph never gets an explanation for the experiences that trouble him. But also like Job, his faith is renewed in the midst of his troubles; he finds an answer to his questions not in some new doctrine or argument about the presence of evil in the world, but in the presence of God in his life.

Surely you place them on slippery ground;
    you cast them down to ruin.
How suddenly they are destroyed,
    completely swept away by terrors!
They are like a dream when one awakes;
    when you arise, Lord,
    you will despise them as fantasies.
. . . .
Yet I am always with you;
    you hold me by my right hand.
You guide me with your counsel,
    and afterward you will take me into glory.
Whom have I in heaven but you?
    And earth has nothing I desire besides you.
        (vv. 18–20, 23–25)

The poem ends with an ecstatic description of Asaph's joy in the renewal of his fellowship with the living God. And we get one of those rare Old Testament glimpses of the promise of heaven, flowering in the midst of the garden of pain. Heaven is not just the place where justice is done, the ultimate payback for the righteous; Asaph's poetry has helped us to understand that, for him, the reward of heaven is the presence of the God he loves and clings to in the midst of this unjust world.

My flesh and my heart may fail,
    but God is the strength of my heart
    and my portion forever. (v. 26)

God sends us his Word in poetry because poetry can reach beyond language to experience—and because it can sometimes reach further and can suggest a mysterious and powerful reality beyond human perception. We encounter this power when we sing hymns of praise, an experience that is becoming more and more the unique domain of Christian worship in a contemporary culture that has lost itself in the maze of materialism. And we encounter this power in God's revelation of himself in Scripture when we read Scripture well with the aid of the Holy Spirit.

Reading the Bible this way, seeing it as the work of human authors working within the literary traditions of their cultures to put word on paper, to communicate the message of God to people, has also inspired me to become a better writer myself. If Luke simply sat at a desk and wrote down words dictated to him by the Holy Spirit he can't be an example to me, but when I read Luke's own account of the process of writing his gospel, his example also moves me to struggle to communicate the message of Jesus Christ to people around me.

> Many have undertaken to draw up an account of the things that have been fulfilled among us, just as they were handed down to us by those who from the first were eyewitnesses and servants of the word. With this in mind, since I myself have carefully investigated everything from the beginning, I too decided to write an orderly account for you, most excellent Theophilus, so that you may know the certainty of the things you have been taught. (Luke 1:1–4)

If I were able to go back in time and speak again to my friend who had decided to read only the Bible, I'd obviously have a lot more to say. I'd tell him that studying literature has made me a better reader, a better writer, a better human being, and a better Christian. More than that, though, I hope I would be able to convince him that part of our calling as Christians is to understand, appreciate, critique, and participate in the gifts that God has given us in our culture and our language. Forty years of study of our literary tradition has only deepened my appreciation for the subject God has called me to teach and deepened my conviction that Christians have been called to steward the resources of English, to love and appreciate our language, and to use it well.

DISCUSSION QUESTIONS

1. What important literary works, other than the Bible, have had a significant effect on the way you think or see the world? How and when did you encounter those works?

2. Think of a work of art that you have experienced both in words and in pictures (script and performance, stage play and film, novel and film). How did the two presentations of the work differ in their form, their message, and their effect? Have you ever liked a film better than the novel it was adapted from or vice versa? Has a film or performance of a play ever changed your interpretation or experience of a written work?

3. Have you read any books that you subsequently wished you had never read? Were these books recommended to you or required in an academic context? What detrimental effect did the book have on you? Have you ever wanted to avoid a book for moral or spiritual reasons and then found it edifying when you read it? Can you identify ways of reading that might help you to read challenging books with more beneficial results?

4. In what ways do you see works of art affecting people around you and American culture in general? Can you think of works that have recently sparked discussions in the media? What have been the content and the general result of those discussions?

5. Make a list of phrases that you hear Christians using frequently. Do these phrases come from Scripture, from theology, or from popular religious discussion? Do these phrases have any meaning outside of the culture of Christianity? Do they clarify or obscure the nature of

God or of our lives in fellowship with him and one another? Can you think of any Christian terms that seem to have come to mean something different in the culture in general from what they mean in the Christian world?

SERIES AFTERWORD

Christians are called to enter, engage, and cultivate every sphere of lawful human activity. And increasingly, in our modern age, this calling requires us to receive training in specialized disciplines beyond the high school level. We must enter colleges, universities, and technical schools to develop knowledge and skills that will equip us to engage in good, even necessary cultural activities in the humanities, the sciences, technology, and the fine arts. But many Christian families are justifiably anxious about sending their children into the modern secular academy to obtain such training; many assume that the norms and beliefs under which the modern academic disciplines operate are at odds with the values their children have been taught in their homes and churches.

While it is important for Christians to instill in one another a biblical framework—a "Christian worldview"—that will help us to understand and interpret what we learn in faithful ways, it is also necessary to consider the fact that the modern academic disciplines are good gifts from a good and gracious God. And they are each packed with insights—"common grace insights"—that can and should be used for the good of the world and the glory of God.

Faithful Learning is a series of modest-sized booklets that provide Christian invitations to the modern academic disciplines. Each volume will introduce students—along with teachers and other educational professionals—to a distinct academic discipline and will challenge readers to grapple with the foundational ideas, practices, and applications found in each of them. The authors of these booklets are highly trained Christian scholars who operate under the assumption that, when understood rightly, each of their disciplines holds the potential for students to cultivate a deeper love for God and for their neighbors. It is our hope and prayer that these booklets will be used by Christians to engage their academic studies with greater confidence and understanding, and that they will thereby be more equipped to *learn faithfully* about whatever pursuit or sphere of human activity God is calling them to.

Jay D. Green

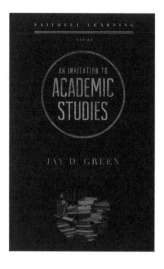

"We were not wrong to learn the alphabet just because they say that the god Mercury was its patron, nor should we avoid justice and virtue just because they dedicated temples to justice and virtue. . . . A person who is a good and a true Christian should realize that truth belongs to his Lord, wherever it is found."
—Augustine, *On Christian Doctrine*

Why study academic disciplines like history, literature, biology, philosophy, chemistry, and computer science? Why even study secular subjects in the first place—especially since we have the Bible to learn from? God has made us to be nonstop learners—and what we learn can actually strengthen our faith! What will *you* learn, and why?

Jay Green invites you to explore the world of academic study, where you will discover vital opportunities to understand and expand God's kingdom. Learn how the church and the academy intersect, and find out how you can cultivate your mind for the glory of God.

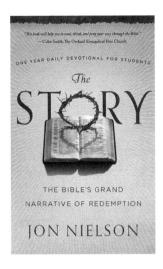

The sixty-six books of the Bible may seem pretty different from each other, but they actually tell one story—a story with one Author, one Hero, and one key plotline.

This yearlong, daily study of God's Word guides you through five acts of his grand story of redemption. Although you won't read *every* chapter in the Bible, daily Scripture and devotional readings will equip you to understand the unity and development of God's story and to grow in your personal discipline of Bible study and prayer.

"Concise, clear, brief readings that will help anyone and everyone deepen their understanding of the big story of the Bible."
—Nancy Guthrie, Author, *The One Year Book of Discovering Jesus in the Old Testament*

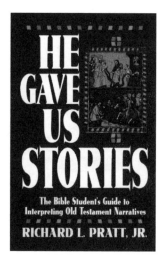

Stories are among the primary means God uses to reveal his truth to us in Scripture. The Old Testament is filled with stories: Noah and the ark, Daniel in the lions' den, Ruth and Boaz—stories of great men and women of God.

What does God want us to learn from these stories? Is there more to them than meets the eye? Richard L. Pratt says yes, and he carefully outlines a method for grasping the wisdom of these ageless narratives. Beginning with the role of the Holy Spirit, he sets forth a three-step process of biblical interpretation.

Pratt is sensitive to the needs of both the beginner and the theological student. He insightfully guides us through considerations of attitudes and orientation, language and history, writers and characters, scenes and events, ancient and modern cultures, and more.

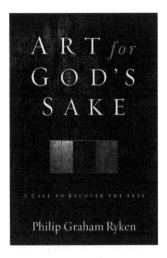

The creation sings to us with the visual beauty of God's handiwork. But what of manmade art? Much of it is devoid of sacred beauty and is often rejected by Christians. Christian artists struggle to find acceptance within the church.

If all of life is to be viewed as "under the lordship of Christ," can we rediscover what God's plan is for the arts? Philip Graham Ryken brings into sharp focus a biblical view of the arts and the artists who make art for God's sake. This is a concise yet comprehensive treatment of the major issue of the arts for all who seek answers.

"Theologically rich and remarkably readable, this book offers sound biblical reasons to cultivate a sense of beauty."
—Nancy Pearcey, author, *Total Truth*

MORE FROM P&R PUBLISHING ON
STUDYING LITERATURE

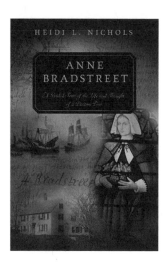

Anne Bradstreet (1612–1669) was America's first published poet. She lived in England and the Colonies during a remarkable historic period market by civil and religious strife and political upheaval.

Bradstreet's life and work challenge stereotypes of Puritans, revealing her vibrant intellectualism and her outspoken love for her husband.

"Nichols not only illuminates the poet's life and social context, she makes it possible for a new generation to savor Anne Bradstreet's own words and to share the sorrows, joy, and hope of her inner journey."
—Charles Hambrick-Stowe, Northern Seminary, Lombard, Illinois